The Bright Dark

For P~

the man at home watering roses in the dark…

The Bright Dark

Poetry of

Stephanie Pilar

Goldfish Press
Seattle

Published by
Goldfish Press, Seattle

2012 18th Avenue South
Seattle, WA 98144

Manufactured in the United States of America

ISBN - 13: 978-0971259843
ISBN - 10: 0971259844

Library of Congress Catalog Card Number 2016935891

Contents

What will you do,
when it is your turn in the field with the god?

Louise Glück
Averno

Spring Again

The air is a sea of sex,
Ah, voluptuous Spring.
The earth, how she seduces.

Went out into the night and
my mouth was filled with fragrances,
the pink magnolia and the dogwood poured their perfumes
and their pollens into me,
when I breathed, when I spoke.

***

By daylight I heard a shout,
"Watch your feet! Violets are coming up everywhere!"
All the inescapable beauties.

Everything is medication for the despair of living, the agony.

Everything on earth can fall apart too fast.

Even our bees are vanishing. Quiet catastrophe. Hives
abandoned. Silence.
In the United States we call it Colony Collapse Disorder.
The English who are suffering a similar decline call it Mary
Celeste Syndrome, after a ghost ship found floating far out at
sea with no crew on board.
Imagine no more pears, no more apples, no more almonds,
no more blackberries, no more honey.

No more honey.

***

I had been tasting my mortality,
It was being fed to me by tablespoons.

Death is always in the air
and in the flowers.

*

You who so love Spring,
may have suffered many winters.

***

Don't you think Hades had to change his routine also?

***

Our days above ground are limited.
All knowledge is incomplete.

In my own childhood, it was so easy to step on snakes,
I grew eyes on my feet.

We have to step somewhere.
 Ah, Voluptuous Spring.

"Rape of Proserpine" by Bernini   Part I.

In a museum full of silent patrons
there is a sculpture in a room with white walls.

A man embraces a woman. He holds
her too tight. Her breath shortens. She drops her flowers.
"This is not ballet," she says. "I want to go home."
All around them the world is black.
"Hush," he says.
He wears a crown but she is not
interested. You can hear her scream
through her hand.   There is
no blood, only cold marble.

His muscles have a life of their own.
He built them out of his own flesh and blood
and now they possess him.
He has fewer choices than one imagines.

She pushes at him, then looks away,
hoping someone might witness this
and send help. Where is her mother?
The earth keeps changing hands.

A dog opens its mouth only to find
its voice has been lost.
It is against the rules to
howl in museums.
There is only
an alarmed silence.

She has lost all gravity.
He has lost all singularity.
It is the end of civilization
          and their beginning.

When I back away, my own eyes released,
I note the museum guard who stands
like a prisoner all day,
a job that was once almost mine.

Beginning

Outside the Hotel, it was the Empress trees,
the Royal Paulownia, the ones with the heart-shaped leaves
which were blooming with fragrant violet flowers.
By coincidence,
new to each other, you and I had both worn lavender shirts,
and it appeared we had fallen from the branches
in a high wind.

We had yet to learn the tree's name or that is was considered
an aggressive ornamental, meaning it knows how to thrive
in many conditions. It adapts,
springs forth from adventitious buds,
survives fire, cutting, bulldozers, gypsy moths.
A fast growing flowering shade tree, with a trunk valued for
crafting furniture and musical instruments.

You touched my wrist lightly
and I put my head on your knee.
We were in the hotel room
as if inside the same compass.
Intending to sleep in separate beds,
this did not happen.
There was not much sleeping either
but a cool fire,
Some other kind of consciousness,
a trance,
as we conjured in each other
fire and stars and night and morning
over and over.

The Hunt

Leaving the computer lab after midnight,
I heard the coyotes howling,
a sound that cut through the skin
like teeth.
They were hunting
on the high hill
above me,

Chasing something perfectly silent,
a panting ghost of its former self.

From where I stood,
I could hear my own heartbeat

and musical though the howling and singing was
I thanked my own lucky stars-(the same ones
that were poking through the night canopy
like the tips of icicles-)

that I was not smaller than the coyote,
that the beautiful eerie song
half celebration, half dirge
was not
the last thing I ever heard.

Email from Mr. Hades

Underground.
He wants me to go back there, underground
with him and he does know how to make
winter look tantalizing, irresistible.
A thing that satisfies a thirst.
Snow white pictures of ducks, feathers sparkling with frost,
a walk along a pond all turned into a sea-green slurpee.
A golden dog reposes in a drift of snow,
glowing like a sun in a cloud.
There are tall bright evergreens with tips spread like fingers
reaching towards me,
all of this intended to make me think
that there is no greater ice queen than my heart.

And I know that I will go,
I've predestined it.
It hardly occurred to me
not to swallow.

Drop

I get lost in my hair which is in your hands and
I feel like the sea kelp
with currents and little fishes hiding and flowing through me
and my thoughts become so calm
that then there are no thoughts.

Other times I know that I snap with impatience,
crocodiles in me surface unexpectedly, the terror is primal.

My body is just many bodies of water.
Your hands are a boat whose oars paddle over me,
skimming and dipping into my surface
turning me into an ecstasy made of light.

The world contained in a drop.

We fell,
as if down a well.

The Joke

I am kneeling in the Acme grocery store in Fair Haven, New
Jersey perusing the dizzying assortment of chocolate chips on
the lowest shelves when an elderly man leaning on his cart
approaches and asks:
"Soup, down the next aisle?"
"Yes, I believe it is."
"Making cookies?" he asks.
"Yes," I smile.
"Small children?"
"Nope, just me. How about you?"
"Nope, at 94 I am on my own."

His eyes are clear and blue and he looks really not even a day
over seventy. Nice skin, straight posture. The only give-away
is the very careful way he grips the cart's hand bar. And the
fact that he is relaxed, he seems to have time, unlike some of
other shoppers who are so hurried we must dodge them like
traffic.

"They had a big party for my 90th" he says.
We continue to chat. He tells me a joke.
"You know what the inside of a tree and a dog's tail have in
common?"
I shake my head no.
"They are both the furthest from the bark."

"Ok," he says, "here is another one:
There was a 90 year old man who went to his doctor and told
him to give him a physical because he is getting married, and
that to his surprise and delight he is marrying a 25 year old.
The doctor says, "I will do it but I am not sure it is a good
idea, it could lead to death."
The man shrugs and says, "Well, if she dies she dies.
What can you do?"

Bronx Zoo

Wild things tower over us.

We cage the carnivore for our entertainment.

Standing on her hind legs and dressed in her golden fur she stood at least ten feet tall. Bigger than imagination. All muscle and gold. It would be a quickie death if she chose you. Thrilling. A one-of-a-kind, once-in-a-lifetime experience, not to be repeated. Perhaps there would be a truly novel and delicious thrill in it, maybe it would feel oddly good. But you wouldn't live to tell of your last moments so no one would ever really know.

She had a soap-opera star name, Sasha or Alexis, but her body was all goddess of fur and teeth and claw and grace. Purity of purpose.

A Bengal, her species seriously endangered, she lives at the Bronx Zoo and three times a day in front an awestruck crowd her keepers offer her an enrichment activity. She is rewarded by being fed meatballs on a stick for showing her paws, lying down, and standing on her hind legs. At the very end, she receives a prize piece of rabbit, skinned and shiny as a piece of chicken we might find in our own kitchens.

Later a tigery moon rises in the sky above us and roars.

Wrens vs. Bluebirds

As I slice the meat I experience a quick moment of being unnerved as the brisket opens for me, something about the texture, and as I insert the garlic cloves I am quite aware that this was once a body, a body that quivered as it lived, a body that hopefully once felt happiness and sunshine on its skin and in its eye.

It had been hard to purchase it, I know no more political place than the grocery store, and I have learned to try to quiet all the voices in my head, for otherwise I would not eat at all. Even so, I hear one voice asking "Would it be easier on the planet to buy the beef or pork? Between the two does it make any difference?" We all know beans and rice are a better choice, but this is a day when I am having meat for dinner. And the brisket looks fresh, juicy, is a nice price, well within my budget for the meal.

I am an unintentional animist. Too imaginative perhaps. The potato speaks in my hand as I send the peeler rushing over it to the rhythm of jazz standards playing on the stereo.
I think nothing more about the meat until it lies glistening below my knife. Even as I seared it in golden oil all I thought was 'How pretty.'

But when I cut into it, I was reminded of the article I read online this morning. About the cannibal in Germany. He advertised on the internet for a victim. Found an adult male who came over, they had sex, he cut the victim's penis off and supposedly both tried to eat it before the victim was stabbed to his death and stored in the fridge for later consumption. I did get stuck on that bit "tried." Was it not a complete success?

In the shower I had a whole dialogue (in my head again) in which I was the German judge upholding the prison sentence of the cannibal, explaining I understand he has a fetish and a craving and he felt he had found a willing victim but to uphold some sense of order in society we would really have to keep him in prison since he still expressed an interest in eating good-looking civilians and we had to presume that people willing to have themselves murdered were suffering from um, mental illness, or perhaps a depression. We hoped he would understand.

So I began to think, we are not the only species to eat our own. Look at our mouths, our teeth, humans are supposed to eat whatever they can find. Most creatures simply eat what they can. And today after reading the news and grocery shopping and cooking beef brisket I was still facing what to do about the cute house wren who was building a nest in the bluebird box. We had not seen a single bluebird in the area but still we hoped. And cute as individuals, wrens are notorious for driving away other birds; the females will attack and knock the eggs of other birds right out of their nests.

Egg Woman

She felt like her belly was full of eggs.
She wanted to protect them.
It was as if this would give her some explicit fulfillment.

There had been her childhood theory that women were
voluptuous padded egg-cartons.
She had played with the frog's clustered jelly universe at the
edge of the mud. She had found blue and brown eggs in
nests, cracked open in the grass. Cocoons hung in dark
corners.

After Spring rains, the world woke up singing.
The ground was made of frogs;
the sky was made of birds.

Insects leapt and crossed their legs and rubbed their wings in
ecstasy.
She wore a red velvet robe and tied it loosely.
He would pull the ties like they were reins.
He stroked her hair from the roots in the crown to the tips
that fell down over her shoulders. His fingers felt like
feathers.

When she dreamed,
the world was a giant nest, a pond, a puddle, a chrysalis,
and she was a woman inside an egg,
with an egg inside of her.

yes

I recall you whispering in my ear
after love at the Empress.
We were all clean white sheets and skin,
a mouth near an ear,

Come away with me.

I smiled thinking how sweet, how funny,
how the right thing to say at the moment,
but of course, never, of course not.

Only there was some other part of me listening,
some other part saying

Yes.

The Bright Dark

Full moon as seen through sycamores
A walk beside a pond, dark quiet waters,
Daffodils.

The whole world is the moon's living room.
A party breaking up on a lawn,
Laughter and the flashlight-like glow of cell phones.

The chemical sweetness of a tree pink in the darkness
Limbs laden with magnolia blossoms,

The golden dog on the long leash,
The man at home watering roses in the dark.

Lesson from the Blind Past

I.

The sun says,
"It has taken me so long to reach you down there
To travel this distance, speed of light even,

That by the time I arrived
Your face in the window was gone."

II.

She fills her eyes
With the sunlight she finds on the pond.

When she turns around
It is too dark to see inside the rooms.

III.

In an earlier life
A blind man once touched her in an elevator.
She uses the memory of her response to guide her now.

Imponderable Night

You moon/ pool of milk
I was your window.
I was your room.

How many times you hatched inside of me.

       ***

Giant moths flap like bats at my night lit windows.
The glass smooth as a mirror reflects the blackness back.
Can we ever see right through ourselves?

       ***

You woke me sitting on the bed in the primordial dark,
your face a timeless clock.
You snuck in the window, as I snuck out.

       ***

You once hung from a tree.
Fruit I did not even desire to pluck.
Lantern hung like a message left by the ancestors.

You are broken on many boughs
and then reborn.

Facing a Window

Facing a window,
my back to the world
I see a reflection within a reflection,

And beyond that, trees
and the shadows of trees.

I have been thinking about the owls
who are breeding now, floating in the air
feather-heavy
feather-light

The ones who release blind snakes into their nests
to keep the parasites in check.
How innovative,
having a living vacuum.

And how many creatures we will never encounter,
And how many microhabitats, like the nest, or the heart.

And what is it like to be the snake, plucked
from the soil, raised high
and deposited in a world above the world you once knew?

I sit here, looking out the window,
at the earth, orbiting the sun.

The Deepest Ground Water

You opened in me channels for emotions
like a man dowsing for water feels his rod bend.
Quivering I felt the rivers rise in me, water
that had been buried deep for centuries,
pushing upwards through rock and stone.

I was pulled to the surface
by the magnetic force of your touch.

What was once quartz turned to water,
wet and hot and sustaining as it pushed through
the network of flesh.

We are full of hot red rivers.
We gush silently.
It is amazing we do not bleed to death
inside ourselves.

No one had dug wells here before.
No one else had risked this drowning.

Looking at Trees with Chen Wu

Bill Chen Wu, Puvin,
When we are walking and looking at trees
it is as if we are in the world's greatest art museum.

We are tireless, and the green boughs of our conversation
are hung with leaves and vines,
and full of nests.
Sometimes a red bird alights
and then flies off.

At the end, the sidewalk goes two ways
and for some reason we cannot name,
we are laughing and laughing and laughing, we are all
laughing,
like a pleasant and musical thunder is rumbling within us.
We say farewell, and part ways,
the laugh now broken into three parts
and carried away with us.

Confession

There were not just pomegranate seeds,
there were also dark chocolate
covered espresso beans.

There was coffee.
At one point there were free cookies.
There was an occasional encounter with authentic
Italian food. Bread from grain, meat from the animal,
salt, rosemary, olives, hunks of parmesan, the first real
pasta carbonara of my life.

I must confess, I feasted.

Part of me knew
it would make it more difficult to return.

Part of me forgot myself,
and in my insatiable hunger, decided the future.

How we weigh ourselves down,
sometimes happily.

Apollo

This time when I saw him
I was not afraid.

His chariot rose up out of the waters,
he was not facing me.

And the Tritons who blew their horns
did not have eyes to see.

The horses broke their breath on the air.

I waited for the moment when
I would be claimed,

My mortality
served on the half shell.

Something in me shivered
and stood still.

Persephone Daphne

It seemed the abduction was over, I no longer heard
the breaking of branches, rumble of clouds, the
earth did not shake and grumble like thunder, the
flowers were no longer dark.
I looked around and could see a stag, moss in his antlers,
over there a female deer and her fawn approached, they
seemed to not notice me
as they bent their heads and nibbled at the earth.
I knew not what I had wished for
and continued to try to find legs so that I could run.

Whom had I told no?

Finally, I realized I had followed Daphne
and stood still.
Small green leaves began to unfold from me.
This was how
        I would go down in the history books,
How I would hold up, my own
                tiny little piece of sky.

I return to you

The jasmine had bloomed
in my absence, your presence.
Nasturtium, tomato, sunflower, sweet pea, morning glory
had all sprouted, twining up in green
to meet the sun.

When the plane sunk down in Newark yesterday,
slipping through the violet air,
descending to the flat line that was the earth
leaving the sun and clouds above,

You were there on earth to meet me.
My head full of clouds and heart full of seeds,
I burst like a piñata
who had been stuffed only with happiness.

Reunion

I call to him to look at the full gold moon in the trees. We
stand there with our arms around each other and he says,

"Life is kind of like the moon, full and perfect and glowing."

And he pauses and then continues,
"for about three days a month."

And he laughed, and I laughed, and we headed to bed.
I in my new purple dress.

Solstice Double Rainbow

Sometimes you think the earth cannot get any more beautiful
and then a double rainbow rises up out of the land and
plunges into the ocean
and four Russian kids in New Jersey leap into the sea,
fearless, riding the waves into shore, bobbing and tumbling
like seals while their mothers stand watch.

And we two strangers look over them also
as the rain and sun falls all around us,
and the sea sweeps in and out,
and into the deep gray sky are burned the colors
violet indigo blue green yellow orange red,
and on the other rainbow mirrored
red orange yellow green blue indigo violet,
Reflective twins, stunt doubles.

No one needs a promise, no one needs a pot of gold.
Everything we need is right here,
and side by side we sink our feet into it
as it rushes in all around us.

Asian Love Affair

Instead of saying I love you,
You just go
and make the rice.

"Rape of Proserpine" by Bernini   Part II.

At last,
I am standing here, in the cool interior of the Villa Borghese
in Rome.
Outside there are lemons swollen with sunshine.
The statue I saw in Los Angeles must have been a replica, a
stuffed hide,
but a clue, a cipher, it abducted me.
This is the real thing. It is still alive.
The beauty and the agony intermingle,
are not the flip sides of the coin
but the lip of the coin.
The part that is considered "the third side"
presses together and like a small round metal ribbon
holds together life and death, the light and the dark, this
currency of female and male, of ascent and descent.
There is really nothing else like this. Preconsensual, the
darkness of fruit falling to earth,
brightness of the open petals of the hand.
His skin sinks into hers. Her skin rises to meet his.
It is not just about surrender.
As they sink, they are rising,
to the heights of the great depths.

The earth claims us, drags us under.
Oh the ecstasy, oh the terror.
It won't be the last time.

"Is this Heaven? Are we in Heaven?"

" No. This is New Jersey."

--Quote from the television show House in which
Hugh Laurie as Dr. House responds to his patient whose heart has
miraculously restarted after being stopped for a day.

It's Spring

It's Spring and
the tiny colored flags appear

marking where the neighbors
have poisoned their grass

as if poison understands property lines
as if this is something to celebrate.

***

And oh god,
the ceaseless mowing.

Trying to Save the Earth from My Yard

Wake up to the Chemlawn van across the street,
"Pesticides," it proudly exclaims in large letters.
The side of the van shows a smiling Dalmatian on a bed of
nuclear green Astroturf
and it is early in the day to be cynical
but I cannot help thinking
'That dog is being poisoned.'

How am I supposed to save the earth from my yard
when you have the Chemlawn guy in your driveway
before I even wake up?

And it is early in the day…

…here in the land of invisible fences.

We are all driving around in our hybrid cars.
Who am I to you,
and who are you to me?

I have not even seen you or gotten to ask you these questions
face- to- face
and now it is so late in the day…

Your grass, how it glows.

Later I learn it is Lily- of- the- Valley

Something is coming up!
Since I am new here
I do not know what it is
but it looks like green newspapers
tightly rolled
rising up out of the earth.

I look forward to reading the announcement.
Should be just a few more days,
I'll tell you when I find out.

Rejuvenation

Fair Haven Fields. Late morning. It was raining.
There were flowers.
Daffodils. Small children who gently pulled Gabe's ears and
stroked his fur. The whole world felt like Easter, like
Passover. Pastel, enduring.

I met my blonde superhero realtor Elaine and her white
westie T-Rex. We promptly met her two friends Emma and
Erik and decided to all walk together in the same direction.
Gabe took such an instant liking to Emma he jumped up on
her as if to give her a hug, something which I have never
seen him do to a stranger. He left a paw print on her thigh. I
apologized and she brushed it off and said, 'Oh no I was
wearing dirty pants. Erik and I have a three month old
puppy.'

The rain fell as tiny beads. Words flowed like water broken
loose from winter glaciers. Conversation was three mountain
streams running downhill and meeting in the meadow.

Her Scottish husband ran on ahead while we chirruped like
birds and the dogs followed.
After one long loop T-Rex was weary but was not limping
like last time.
Elaine said she would call us to go to the chocolate shop.
We caught up to the running husband.
Erik mentioned Keats. Asked if I liked art.
Together they told me about their first date when Emma was
left waiting.
She gave him another chance.

I inquired about their home in Rhode Island where they
spend summers. Like Eva's house it was built in the 1700's
and has not only history but a ghost.
Emma has heard it but Erik snores so loudly he scares it off.

Emma confided she had had a panic attack and found
adjusting to life in NJ was hard after many years abroad. She
missed Europe where she walked everywhere and rode her
bicycle.

I came home filled with happiness. I had happiness and it
fully had me.
Rain, engaging conversation, a long walk in woods...
Spring had arrived.

It overflowed with promises it would not keep.

Easter, New Jersey

In a land of chocolate crosses, I eat a coconut cream egg
because I no longer know what to believe about Jesus. My
own lover is Buddhist. He bites into the leg of a dark
chocolate bunny rabbit. Gently. For the holiday we walk
around a nursery admiring tall blue spruce trees. We survey
the ground we will open up so the spruce roots can penetrate.
We hang a bluebird box on the back fence. We take the dog
for a walk at the ocean and I find a place where the stones are
being swirled around by the hands of the ocean, in the palm
of the waves, their edges worn off. Smooth round stones like
moons or mints. Tiny orange whelks. Soon my back pocket is
full of round rocks and my front pocket is full of tiny shells. I
am a thief. I walk around collecting artifacts from my good
times.

May 16th

Out walking the dog around the pond, I hear a vehicle pulling up behind me. It is the mailman, a mailman I have never seen before and he is waving a milk-bone biscuit. So I stop in someone's yard and the mailman pulls over and leans out of the truck and gives the crunchy bone-shaped biscuit to Gabe and then the mailman gets all the way out of the truck and gives Gabe a full body massage, running his fingers through Gabe's feathery fur, examining his frilly soft ears and feet, saying these creatures are god's gift to humans, the best dogs ever, and it turns out he used to breed them but no longer does though he has the sire and the dam and two puppies still. I can see through his graying hair that he has a flesh colored lump on his head which must be some sort of tumor and so I am wondering if he is being conscious to savor every day or if he was always like this, as I listen to his enthusiastic recommendation to find someone with a boat any boat even a duck boat and to go on out to Starvation Island off of the end of Rumson Road and just let the dog out there to run and run.

Dulce de Leche

Went to see Cookieman at the bakery. The café Tavolo Pronto opened this Spring and it was like having a little outpost from Italy land in the neighborhood. Giant cheeses hang from the ceilings. Cookieman's real name is Dan but I call him Cookieman because he has always given me something sweet for free. It began the first time we met. A lemon drop, a pignoli cookie, some chocolate bark. Without even knowing it was my birthday, that day he chose to make little personal-sized dark chocolate cakes, some topped with raspberry preserves and some with nutella. I bought one of each. He always asks where I have been and sometimes I have to say nowhere but this time I said Rhode Island. He was making a new kind of cookie. Alfajores. Chilenitos. A South American cookie, two round scalloped butter sugar cookies held together by dulce de leche and dusted with powdered sugar. His ex girlfriend's recipe, he says. I say "Oh you should make a cookbook of recipes of ex girlfriends." He says "Oh it would be very short, only two pages." I tell him that his café is my church. He says I should come there more often.

Last time it came at you

Last time it came at you, you recognized it,
and dodged it, this time it wore a mask of
flowers, your heart was a typical bee,
dipped in blindly, your
stinger was no defense,

Lying on the sidewalk writhing,
oh the agonies of the pollen,
gravid with gravity

Weighed down so heavily
with your harvest,
you cannot make it home.

Sea Gull, Union Beach NJ

I love the seagull in his little grey coat. He looks dressed up
as if for a fancy party, only now I think he is waiting for the
clouds to look right, the way humans wait for the right bus to
come.
He wants to take to the skies,
though he is torn
because sometimes there are French fries here,
even though the sign warns humans
that it is against all the rules to feed the gulls.

Everyone is on their lunch break all at once,
nature and its people and its little winged things.
The fries go so nicely with clams.
He heads out and disappears over the whitecaps
as if called away,
back to some kind of work.

Across this water,
the twin towers are missing.

On Watching 24 with the New Boyfriend

I did not know that they would do this,
kill off the loyal character you loved most,
the one who was there through thick and thin,
with the long suffering eyes, the round belly,
the one who always worked hard,
the one who never got the girl.

My new boyfriend and I now find ourselves
engaging in ritualistic Monday night television watching
eating ice-cream floats while the world goes to hell
for an hour, and then is saved
just in the nick of time, over and over again.

But this week when the nerve gas canister leaks,
the Unthinkable happens, the unsung hero is trapped,
outside the safe zone,
and there is no commercial break
during which he escapes
or is rescued.

I lay down a new law,
I cannot watch anymore.
If he is not worth saving,
What hope is there for the rest of us?

We are terrified in our own living room,
and yet, we cannot tear our eyes off the screen,
not even to look at each other.

Dress Code

It's the kind of place you routinely see women in pink
jogging suits
even orange ones
even purple

even brown velour like a furry chocolate bear suit.
This looks good on some people.
This is something you would not know
if New Jersey did not exist.

The first time I happened upon a man wearing an entirely
dark business suit, dressed as if a banker in a meeting,
walking the sandy beach midday, smoking a cigar,
speaking with some animosity into his cellphone, ignoring
me but to raise his eyebrow in passing, I thought I had fallen
into a Mafia movie. 'This is really happening,' I thought.
'This is Real.'

I swallowed his smoke, the salt air, the sound of gulls.

Serenade, Marinade

Do you ever have that experience where one minute you and your mate are cheerfully looking each other in the eye over the dinner table and a few minutes later you realize there is a distance between you that will never be bridged? Suddenly the other person is talking to the dog and you are not the jealous type but it almost seems like they are flirting and you are alone on an island.

But you have built this life together, as if from driftwood and what has been salvaged from all past shipwrecks, and it took the two of you to bring dinner to the table, steaks from the grill marinated all day, sautéed asparagus, a deep green salad with ripe red tomatoes and cucumbers from the garden.

Regular Coke for one and a diet Pepsi for the other. Decadence of ice. Of choices.

What happened to those people who moments ago were humming along in a natural harmony, so anchored in the mundane, that siren's serenade. Where did they go?

And now you are adrift. Your bare feet feel the grit on the floor, as if someone has built your life on sand.

Shipwrecked

Shipwrecked,
I hold onto
my idea of
who I am

like it is a log
floating on an
ocean.

Soon I will reach a shore

you can only get to
by drowning.

Calling the Police on the Geese

I see animal control here, an ominous white van,
I get a bad feeling.
Each day when I wake or get out of the shower,
something else has happened.

Something is missing: a tree, three ducks, and now maybe the
geese and their goslings.
Next thing, maybe us too. Maybe we will wake up tomorrow
and find ourselves missing.

Suburbia is so well-ordered. Who can know all the rules?
People push a button; they want a certain thing to happen.
I too have my wants; I want everything to be left as it is,
at least until we come up with a better plan.

Wait, now the police are here too. Why? They are walking at
the babies from different directions, the birds scatter like
loose feathers. But then animal control and the policeman
shake hands with such a polite and lovely gesture, in a hey
bro kinda way, I feel better, and even better still when the
policeman stoops to pick up the litter, some beer cans and a
cardboard box. Teens are out for summer. Now I feel a relief.
How short lived will it be?

New Jersey is covered in trash and the best litter I ever saw
was a "Do Not Litter" sign washed up in the kelp amongst
the cans and trash at Sandy Hook National Seashore.

I don't even care that much about Canada geese
but can't anyone leave anything alone?

Every day I wake up and something is missing from the
world.

Suburbia is a kind of ceaseless anxiety. Hold your breath.
Keep holding it.
No one can ever be rich enough. Safe enough.

Did the same man who threatened to call the police on me for
feeding the ducks,
call the police on these geese and their four babies?

Or was there a different man?

The goslings are adorable and all day I watch people pull
over in their cars to watch them eat, plucking the grass like it
is the source of all nutrition and happiness.
This morning a woman and three children were doing a
project at the picnic table and the three white ducks slept
below their feet like puppies.

The van and the police car move on.
I exhale.

There are better wars to fight.

Our Tax Dollars at Work

I lost many friendships by coming here. When it came time
to take the train, I was ill, and almost found god lying there
on the floor. When the rains came I was surprised for I had
left behind the rainy place that was home in my bones, and
gone east, which is where the sun begins, some say.

Last night the dream was that I was shot by terrorists, and I
could so clearly feel the blood that was in my face and hair, a
sea of blood, and my consciousness going under,
but then I was not dead, had not been killed, I only had a
bullet lodged in my throat.

I spent the rest of the dream looking for a doctor who could
remove it.
My mother helped me.
Before the surgery happened, I woke up.

So many wars going on daily
while we shop for the right medical professional.

Playing Cards with the Handless Maiden

I had been playing cards with the handless maiden. She
wasn't a bad player
but you could see it was kind of hard for her, and
I must admit, I found it rather distracting, the way she ended
at the wrists.
It was usually up to me to shuffle.
And there was some guilt, I thought "Why her? And not
me?" I entertained fantasies
of killing people who lop off other people's hands,
even as I tried to keep my attention on
the paper royalty.

Kings, queens, jacks, aces.
Hearts, diamonds, spades, clubs.

Ok ok, it is true.
I was playing Solitaire.

I had to deal for us both.

***

Later I would find in the forest,
the moon's silver gloves.

Coast Guard Rescue

Walking the sand at the Atlantic at sunset
we watch a small Coast Guard boat float and bob beneath the
full moon
and reflect the last pink splash of daylight.

When they detach a smaller boat from their starboard side
and then back away from it, we watch from shore and I feel a
slight panic
not understanding what is going on. Will we be called upon
to swim out and assist? Has something gone wrong?

But soon it is obvious that they are practicing, enacting
something dramatic,
as they don their orange vests and floatable gear and I give
such deep thanks
for the men and women who are preparing to rescue us in the
future.

Waiting in Line

I am waiting in the grocery store line glancing at magazines
mainly curious if Angelina Jolie has given birth in Namibia
while the checker and a glamorous but aging lady with big
black curls, movie star hair, chats elegantly, really she had a
way of chatting that was elegant, like her hair.

She has not had plastic surgery, she is like an old time
celebrity, all dressed in black, her face strong and lean, you
know she either has spent years in the theater
or made the world around her a theater.
She says everything with a gesture
and she is magnanimous, you can feel it.

The checker and the lady chat a long time and I do not mind
a bit. You see I am unemployed so time is not money
and the ladies are funny.

Even though the topic is cancer, the checker has had a
hysterectomy,
and now needs a root canal,
they find the humor in this.

The lady says her own doc got a flu shot and now he has the
flu. She must send him flowers.

'What color is his condo?' she asks his staff and they say
'Oh you know, bachelor black and white.'
So she says, 'Well I better not send him any of my Victorian
colors
or he will send them right back to me.'

Chocolate-Covered Vanilla Marshmallows

At the Food Town grocery store in Red Bank New Jersey, I
watch the butcher with the hugely bloody apron stick his
hand into the bulk bin of chocolate-covered vanilla
marshmallow bars,
and while you might think I would find this a deterrent
instead I find myself irresistibly attracted to these strange
oblong confections,
and completely willing to abandon the Jordan almonds whose
pastel sugar shines beneath the fluorescent lights.

By the way in which the large man with the bear like paws
goes for the
chocolate covered vanilla marshmallows I figure they must
be irresistible.

I think he was stealing them.

A minute later, I watch him talking to a lady, his whole white
outfit covered in blood and meat juices, telling her
confidently about the way a cow is cut into pieces
and I wonder where he had hidden the candy, maybe in those
large deep pockets, and usually I buy meat here but today I
buy none.

Instead I buy a single vanilla marshmallow bar.

I am always looking for something to sink my teeth into.

In the privacy of my own home, I take it out of the bag.

It was stickier than I imagined it would be.

It sort of bit back, I didn't even like it at first,
so fake tasting as it touched the tongue, like wax or grease,
but it left such a sweet aftertaste, like living in nature, as if
living off campfire s'mores was ones actual life, the life that
one longed to get back to.
And I could see how if I worked in that building, like a bear
raiding the honeybee's hive,
I might end up going back for more,

and then for more.

The Baby Snow Crab

Even the smallest of creatures carries a sun in its eyes,
Antonio Porchia

It was tumbling there in the surf, fumbling, a creature on the
wrong side of the tracks,
the white foam wall like a death sentence.

It was green, about the size of my hand, and looked like a
little alien.

I always associate them with the deeper seas up near Alaska,
not the Jersey Coast, but here it was, upside down and
waving ten prickly legs,
and it probably did not associate me with its neighborhood
either.

Of course I went to it and tried to make right by righting it,
gently, with my foot.
It grabbed the sand and began clawing a little handhold.
Then the next wave came, and it lay upside down.

I watched and then righted it.
The beach was full of seagulls wearing their finest dark
jackets of feathers,
looking meditatively out to sea.

The crab flailed quietly when the next wave came and
pitched it close to shore,
so I approached, and lifted the creature into my palm.

Easier to avoid its claws than the writhing horseshoe crabs
we had helped tip back over during mating season, this crab

seemed so defenseless, a little baby, not like the snapping
claws of the blue crab who intimidates
and yet whose shells litter the beach.

I was surprised by its texture, I expected something crisp but
the crab felt soft like a beanbag or a frog's belly.

I pitched it low and long so it landed just past the waves.
I was not sure it would survive,
but I stuck around, hoping it had sunk and swum.

The ocean is by definition
a very large solution.

I was relieved when it did not wash up onto the beach again.

Late Night Walk with Scissors

Someone had thrown the sun in the trash,
left the Indonesian ornament curbside for pick-up,
so I came by and picked it up.

This world confuses me and sometimes I think I live
underground
and sometimes above ground, and sometimes in the sky, and
that this world is a Black Orpheus movie and
that on the other side of the earth they have more sense
than to throw away the sun.

It was as if I had found Sylvia Plath's great grandma's trash
pile
or even her own trash pile had she lived long enough to find
the poetry in aging.
There was enough stuff on our curbs to make a Mardi Gras
float.

Who throws this stuff out?
It looked like all the ghosts of Christmas past had unloaded
their sleighs.
Haven't these people ever been in our own third world
country?
I fantasized about driving the stuff to the inner city of
Camden, Trenton, Newark,
where every day is not a holiday for those who wake up
there.
I just heard that the prostitutes are making only five dollars a
job.

I came home with a glass dome and a sun.

Yes, the bell jar has a little crack in its top
but who doesn't?

Tonight I am going back with scissors,
 to rescue what I can from the piles by the curbs

because who doesn't need
a perfectly good
broken sun?

Three Mall Scenes

Shirt for Sale

New Jersey: Because Hell was Full

Shirt on a Teenage Boy at the Monmouth Mall

Let's flip a coin:
Heads I get tail
Tails I get head

Death Penalty

They go running through the mall
And the mother calls out to her daughter,

"Do *not* grab a lollipop,
Penalty of Death,
Ok?"

Fried Oreo

Having never tasted one but seeing a sign for them and liking the novelty of new but not high adrenaline experiences, I decide that I must have one. It is the Blues and Jazz festival on the water in Red Bank NJ, advertised as the largest free music festival on the East Coast and indeed I am impressed at how the narrow strip of land has been transformed. But it seems the rain has been missing its tunes because it shows up in buckets and a hearty few are dancing but mainly there are people under trees and umbrellas and everywhere mist and mud. My mate and I stand under a sycamore juggling iced tea and umbrella and camera while trying to eat bbq pork with some degree of decorum. Two young punk men take refuge under the branches with us. The teenager facing me is dressed all in black with shiny spiked hair and dimples and piercings in the soft parts of his face. He is holding a plate of what look like small batter fried Frisbees covered in powdered sugar and I say, "Excuse me, but what are those?" And he smiles disarmingly and says, "Fried Oreos," and offers the plate my direction in the rain and says, "Would you like one?"

Happiness

Tiny thing, happiness,
no bigger than a human heart
or fist, or palm.
We must nurture it when we find it
broken-winged chick
we cup our hands around
with an eggshell-thick hope
we might protect it, somehow,

Shade it from the very same
inside-out blue umbrella sky
from which it fell,
that gravity free place
to which it must return
if it is ever to mean anything,
or get anywhere using its wings.

We fulfill our destinies
while the garbage trucks rumble by.

Summer Poem

He has put out cherries for Buddha, in a little blue dish.
They look delectable, and I must remind myself to resist
them.
I am not so good at resisting things.
My lover is the fresh green grass I run through barefoot.
I fall down in him, laughing, and my red dress gets drenched
with dew.

FedEx Man

Every day I see FedEx man
eating his lunch in his truck
at the park.

I imagine he is a dreamer like me
and we come to share this dream
this lunch break where we can imagine
that in these green fields
lined by trees,
we are free.

Coney Island Part I.

I was 17 and you were dying of AIDS,
  I have to say dying of
  because it was the 80's
and one couldn't even get a diagnosis,
  much less a cure.

You'd be gone by Valentine's Day.

That summer we raided the library like pirates
and lay in the thick green grass across the street from
the train station converted to a pizza parlor

Like my own personal Ian McKellan you
 read Ferlinghetti to me,

And he
a little charleychaplin man
who may or may not catch
her fair eternal form
spreadeagled in the empty air
of existence

and so today
twenty years later when I am living in Jersey and going to
visit Coney Island before it
disappears like a lost city,
not under ash or ocean or sand but under condominiums,
I can hear you in my head reading, *A Coney Island of the
Mind*
like you never died.

Coney II.

We went looking for mermaids along the shore
It was the last weekend of summer. I wore a blue dress.

We wanted Nathan's hotdogs and postcards, to stroll like
tourists on mini holiday
though we were only an hour from home.

Who knew twenty years ago that I would live an hour away
from this place, Rabbit Island

Where everyone is either taking photographs
or being photographed.

The rain comes down, a sputtering piss.

Once the clouds are empty, once the sky is spent
the sunshine opens its umbrella.
We glow like candy beneath it.

The world may not last forever.

The Walrus
Coney Island Aquarium

The walrus at the NY Aquarium has a strange almost human affect, like a gigantic Yul Brynner with his huge head, his whiskery smile, his bright eyes.

And not only can you see him up above the water like a wrestler sitting in a hot tub
but you can go below where when he is done sitting he is very busy hanging upside down and pressing against the glass and entertaining all the kids,
before swimming off again.

At one point he does a very impressive display with his penis and flippers and while
it could be territorial it really instead seems like a great expression of happiness and joy, like swimming and exposing oneself feels quite good.
Better than anything.

We are all immigrants here,
not sure of the customs.

Ah nature, wouldn't you like to be it.

Every Once in A While and When You Least Expect It

"I'm going to hold you every once in awhile, and when you
least expect it,"
the father said to his young daughter, there at the New Jersey
State Fair at the Sussex County Fairgrounds on a hot day in
August 2007.
She turned her happy back to him and wandered just ahead of
him, taking in the sights.
And I thought this man has just become my hero,
the father many never have.

The State Fair, the people packed tight in the heat, hands full
of snow-cones and iced drinks, ice-cream cones melting
down their arms, pizza and hotdogs, cotton candy and candy
apples,
Looking at the Jacob's goats with the four old-world horns,
the fat she-cows and the panting sheep, a bull having his fur
spray painted an even darker black until he was a velvet
darling with a gold ring in his nose.
Chickens wore white like a down pillow had burst and been
glued to them. There were roosters the size of children.
Bunnies lay on their sides leaning against frozen water
bottles. Chicks hatched under a light, every few hours.

There were rides, places you could go that defied gravity.

We had eaten two funnel cakes before the day was over.

And all day I had carried with me the man who would lift his
daughter, as he said,
"Every once in a while and when you least expect it."

You can find such love there at the fair,
amongst the cows and the one elephant
who carried the kids all day in a lumbering circle.

Long Branch, NJ

Waiting at the train station
I step over a melted ice-cream cone
left long ago, sticky and thick on the concrete

Can't figure out why I feel punched in the eye
maybe I slept wrong
maybe something heavy-handed in my dreams

I'm chilly waiting on this bench
like the summer heat cannot penetrate me
now that I am becoming so thick-skinned.

My own peach bonbons spill
into the bottom of my purse.
Things seem to be losing themselves.

Cinco De Mayo

The news reports that there are over 400,000 illegal
immigrants in NJ,
the 7th largest immigrant population in the US.

A local NJ radio show has a devilish program called "La
Cuca Gotcha"
in which they are advocating people turn in illegal Latinos,
a contest ending on Cinco De Mayo.

On an airplane from Seattle to Newark,
I use all my inner strength to not stab the man sitting behind
me in the head with my plastic fork.
He has summoned the stewardess, a brown woman herself,
and asked, "Why are the news subtitles in Spanish?"

She explains that he can listen to the audio in English.
He replies, "The last time I checked, English was the
language of America."
He claims he has no headset.

She walks away. I imagine plunging my plastic tines
into his shiny head. Instead I turn and make my offer,
"Would you like me to pay the two dollars for your headset?"
He says no.
I grip my fork and say, "I have a really difficult time
listening to anyone
say such racist things."
He says "It's not racist."
I say "Yes, it is."
He says "What, are you Spanish?"

Plane Ride II.

On the plane
a boy reads Dostoevski,
marks passages with his
pink highlighter.
The man next to me
has been traveling for over a
day-Delhi to Seattle
and when you ask him
anything he pleasantly replies,
"Sure, sure,"
and falls back asleep.

Each day its own eternity

A splotch of moon

like someone threw some paint
or their pillow
up into the black sky

hangs above the gold Buddha
who sits in the window.

Each day its own little eternity.

Peony

Earwigs
and tiny yellow spiders

Universe the size
and shape
of a bright pink peony
on a stem

plucked from our garden.

Deforestation: the Door to Hell

Earlier I had seen a great bumper sticker-
it read 'Deforestation: the Door to Hell.'

I was driving in my old Honda
and next to me the young man in his new hybrid car
was smoking a cigarette and the smoke
was pouring out his window,
so much smoke that I closed my window,

part of me laughed.
I was on the cell phone

and telling an old friend in Hawaii
that when I was just in Virginia
I saw flocks of cardinals
beautiful red birds

but that all the pine trees in Virginia are
being cut down at once.

Alarmed, I asked my friend
"Where do these people expect the birds to live?"

"In their cars," answered my friend,
"in their cars."

Tooth

I pulled myself
like a tooth.

No wonder I feel so odd
and useless.

One of me is not enough.

Thank you New Jersey

I just want to thank you for this stretch of ocean,
low tide and a long expanse of sand
no other humans in sight between the black boulders
of the jetties.

It is like my own private property,
this Autumn Wednesday between 2 and 3 pm.

And how is this possible, in the most densely populated state
in the nation? More densely populated than Tokyo? Where is
everybody?

But I don't really want to know. I am not complaining.
Thank you for this.

And thank you Sea Bright
for the Free Parking.

Van Gogh

The sky comes in, in waves,
the clouds attached, by strings, to the earth.
Winds brushing the heavens
into an impressionist painting,
as if God were
Van Gogh.

One Year Anniversary

a.

It was the anniversary,
One year, and it wasn't that we weren't speaking
Just that our bodies had taken time off
Lilacs were showing tight purple clusters
And tulips had opened rejoicing
But we were closed like cabinets
Where the salt and sugar sleep.

b.
I think after a year we looked at each other and thought
'Who is this person?'
'How did we get here?'
The pure chemistry of love and sex and newness and magic
had subsided and with a slight sense of shock we could look
around to see
where we were standing and who was standing next to us.
We were new,
like people who were birthed directly into adulthood.

Middle Class, Sort of

Having achieved a certain level of comfort,
I found I was terribly uncomfortable.

The Halibut

I would have to labor for two hours to afford this side of her
body which without its skin weighs just under a pound.

She has been stripped from the sea and scaled.
Her ocean smarts are gone.

Down my hatch she will go,
after baking and gentle brushing with pesto.

To eat her oceanic body is to eat
16.99 a pound and the comfort that it has been determined
that she was harvested
in a sustainable way,
only I realize she might not think so.

Nor would her grandkids who would never be born.

Shouldn't it cost me a small fortune
since it cost her her life?

I overhear the girl in Whole Foods say wistfully,
"I want a life but I don't even know
 what I would do with it."

Kicking the Fish

What I mainly remember was his yellow rubber boots
the gray waves, gray sky, and the purple face
of the puffer fish gasping for breath.

The Latino fisherman was kicking him back to sea
after catching him and reeling him in.

I knew it was all more complicated than it looked
but that it was mainly cloudy anger reflected on my face.

In response his friend came over and more gently moved the
fish with his own foot, back into the sea.

I kept thinking about deportation, how these men might live
in fear
and how they probably actually usually eat what they catch
this is not just a sport
but everybody hates somebody.

It reminds me now of the deer with the plastic Halloween
pumpkin attached to its head.
The deer in the news all week, some concerned citizens
deciding finally they would tranquilize it and free it so it
would not die of starvation,
but could be returned to the wild,
just in time for hunting season.

This is our human nature,
divided inside us
divided outside us.

Dearly Deported

Because we didn't have the first 47 years, we had today,
we lived differently than we would have
had we been from the same small town,
the same continent or coast even.

Recent newspaper articles remind me that
we are blessed at least that immigration officials
will not tear us apart, deporting one of us in the night,
telling us we can reapply for citizenship, for belonging,
in another ten years.

Autumn Equinox

This is day 22 of our happiness,
Our relationship-shaped bliss

It is the autumn equinox
We pledge to go dormant together

And still be there in the spring
When the green shoots rise up

Tentacles first, tentatively
Snug in our husks.

Cookie Man II.

Cookie Man is standing in front of a gigantic silver bowl filled with apples and cinnamon. It looks like a fairytale amount of work. Does someone behind the scenes chop those apples for you? "You are looking at him," he says. How long did that take? "Oh it is the peeling that is the hard part." Do you have blisters? He shakes his head no. "But" he says, "it was thirty apples and it took about twenty minutes." He starts his day at 4:30 am when I am just hitting my own life saving REM. His is truly the Night Kitchen I visit in the afternoons. We end the meal of our conversation talking about bread that is made with walnut and figs.

Our Own Survival

We take walks at the beach, the cold sea comes up to meet
us.
In the distance, New York City glows orange and pink since
the sun passed it by.

Do we need to go all of these places we think we need to go?
It is winter and the roads and runways are slippery.

A seagull picks at a baby shark the surf brought in.
Who knows who broke its neck but it lies lifeless,
becomes lunch for the living still unbroken thing.

We walk by and notice so much and do so little,
because what is there to be done really?

On a winter's day when the world is this cold,
we are focused like other animals on our own survival.
Nothing more, nothing less, than our own survival,
with our breathing that hangs like ghosts in the icy air.

To Itself Even

The world looks like it is made of wet glass,
of infinite icicles,
everything sparkly and shiny and treacherous and

it's like thunder or someone rolling garbage cans or sudden
gunshots.
Cracks and shouts from the trees who are falling,
"Timber!" the ice yells, and then there is a moment of silence
as the tree tumbles down on itself,
cushioning its own fall.

The sky and earth collide.

I look up, one less leafy head above us, one less branch
between us and the stars.

I grieve and duck and dodge and sidestep.
How fast and ruthless nature can be
to itself even, to itself.

Child Artemis Practices Her Craft in the Moonlight
around Christmas Time

I saw Artemis out there under the full moon last night.
Child Artemis she was aiming her new Xmas bow and arrow
at the plastic reindeer. She bagged quite a few and so if you
see
them no longer raising their sparkling electric heads you will
know why.

She was serious in her task, and I must tattle, that just before
dawn rolled in,
in the last blue chariot light of night, I saw her pierce a
plastic Santa,
and giggle and move on.

I can see now that it is stuck there like Cupid's arrow in his
chest
and I am careful that he does not see me, so that he might fall
in love
with the postman instead.

The Merry-Go-Round

The earth is spinning.
You find a place from which to hold on,

I hold on near you.

For now, we hold on from New Jersey.

Do not be afraid to suffer.

...Rilke

Shadowing Hecate

I become keeper of the dogs.
I hold my lantern high.
At night it is like the trees have souls
and are baring them.

All the roads are crossroads.

What moon is that in an orchard of stars?
Melting like wax as it makes its journey,
reaches its zenith, and falls through
the sky, a flowering nightshade.

I use my body to push through the darkness.
The night parts like curtains made only of fog.
The stars are clustered like Queen Anne's lace
And the moon a little sliver of gold.

I only have so many hours left.
(There are only so many hours left.)

Come, let's go.
(You may follow.)

Your Joy

Dog, I wonder what it is like to be you,
all fur and wonder, eyes like amber
the happy sap of centuries.

I shadow you to see how it is done.

You seem so easily pleased.
I toss a porkchop to you and you dance in the bright snow
like a lover has landed.

When your nanny arrives at the window you pee the floor
with happiness.
Laughing I run for the paper towels of modernity
but how much does it matter?

I hardly scold you
for who am I to deny you your joy?
I am still learning.

We have been taught that we must achieve enlightenment
if we wish to stop reincarnating.
You make all possibilities
but the here and now
seem irrelevant.

Your happiness is old, like the sun
but starts new each day, like the sun

And sometimes I feel so very tiny,
but you small thing
are the center of the sun dial, the gnomon
telling us what time it is within ourselves.

Without you the doorstep and the garden would be dark.

You are the golden animal catching light,
making honey of the day,
buzzing with a thousand blossoms to visit,
your face covered in Spring mud.

Your heart made of rabbits.
As you orbit around your toys,

retrieving the round ball,
Who says you are not a god?

Cookie Man III.

It was a long winter, like a deep cold coma. I went into the café hoping Dan could make me the usual iced mocha of happiness. It had been months. He was not there. I picked up my Siciliano panini, a brownie, a honey pecan bar and asked the girl if she knew Dan. "I don't know. I'm new here. I don't think he's here anymore. It's just me and Gino and the guys you see in the kitchen." I tried to order an iced mocha anyway.
But, they were out of chocolate.

I spoke to the man who had been there since Tavolo opened. He smiled and I smiled and in this shared smiling I assumed we had an understanding. "We are open seven to seven," he says. "Sorry lady, little English." "Dan?" I inquire simply. He calls out to a woman entering, "Hello Signora."

I walked through the parking lot, pollen blowing into my eyes. Returning to my car I find that someone has smacked into my side mirror, bending it against the vehicle. I eat my lunch under the cherry trees, sitting in my car with the door open. The panini was good,
but the world was not the same.

Previously

I had to walk two years to get to you.

There were smooth stones along the way, but the way was
lonely. I was fortunate
to have prepared many sandwiches, to carry bread and
cheese, the world provided water.

There were streams where I waited for my turn after the
bears and lions and other cats. Once I saw a bright gold fish
swimming in the pool from which I drank. Once high in the
mountains there was a silver trout with a rainbow for its skin.

I did not know that I would find you;
only that it was my job to walk.

When the house collapsed there was nothing else to do.

Barn's burned down
Now I can see the moon.
                        Masahide

I do not know if I should tell you
about all the little ouches along the way.
They seem to make you flinch.

We have all suffered.

Just when we thought we could settle in, the world shifted
again.

Death arrived like the last telegram ever sent,
and somehow it was addressed to us.

Box of Broken Angels

A box arrives in the mail.
The return address is from a beloved friend
and the tears of happiness well up in me,
because for one moment in my mind
this box contains that initial seed of our friendship,
a lemon the size of a grapefruit,
she had mailed to me fifteen years earlier.

I come to my senses, knowing she has died.
Her daughter- in- law has been boxing up contents of the house,
encloses a kind note, she wanted me to have these.

I know the ceramic angels were not broken when they left Colorado
and began flying to New Jersey
but somehow the fact that they have lost their wings
on this final journey is fitting.

I myself have never felt so earthbound.

When they reach me they are still smiling
but their wings and sometimes arms are separate from them,
rattling like loose change.

I recognize one of them as a souvenir from the last time
my friend and I went to Cripple Creek
to relive a moment of glory at a casino where you once put in a nickel
and the world lit up and threw its dazzling money at you.

I think I can put the angels easily back together
though I see no real purpose in trying,
for the one I would tell the triumphant tale

has gone on and left this tragic tea party.

Washing my face in cold water,
I am left thinking about all the fabrics I stain,
the way my tears must contain my DNA.

The way her earthly life was left
but I am here bearing the imprint of our friendship,
a word which barely says anything.

Five Blue Shirts

A full moon over a pond and the world
looks like Christmas, a blueish glow in the air
I associate with a happiness spent in childhood.

Today I made gingerbread from your Mom's recipe.
You know I dreamed she was not yet gone.
We knew that she was leaving,
but still she entered the room smiling,
carrying five freshly washed and folded blue shirts.

Using up the Last of the Gravity

The pale golden dog sleeps at my feet
while purple lightning splits the sky with
its toothy axe.
Crack, the thunder slams its flat hand down on the world.

The dog sinks deeper into the floor
demonstrating how it is to hug gravity hard.
I watch the world light up
and then disappear.

I do not know that he will be dead
before the next season of storms.

Death in July

Everything we loved was stopping breathing
It was getting hard for us to breathe.

The air was thick, it was like trying to
Breathe through sweat, through fog.

The air was a jungle of agony.

We stifled our screams.
Our tongues were useless
   like single feathers.

It Came Again

It came
It swept out the marrow in our bones

You would have thought the sky was full
of cackling witches and a glowing moon
covered in cobwebs

But it was eerie and silent and vast.

Everything seemed hollow.
We would have welcomed
something as substantial as a black cat
crossing our path

Something as animal as that.

Instead we were left realizing how thin
the human skin,

How long it lasts before it lets
the nothingness of everything
rush in.

The fifth death

After this one I stopped waiting for the other shoe to drop
and just expected constant hail on the roof.

You stop cringing
but you also give up a little.

No sense cleaning the house again
if a fire will be sweeping through tomorrow.

Upside Down

After the fifth death, the order of which deaths were the most
shocking
and the hardest to endure rearranged in order.
Some of them just left us still in a state of eerie disbelief,
we would deal with those later.

Some left me weeping when I could not pick up the phone to
reach the deceased,
when letters did not arrive, when the world got so small and
dark and no one
was reflecting light back from outside this cave.

And the dog who died? We missed him the deepest in that
preverbal
joy of running- in –the- fields- at-the -beginning –of-time
primal innocence sort of way.

I turned his photos upside down, so he appeared to not be
rolling on his back
in the grass, but running along joyfully with the green fur of
the planet upon him
and his feet, treading the stars.

Sunday Phone Calls

On Sundays I used to call my grandmother
but she is no more.
There is no one there to call.

I have been having a lot of nightmares
and I am laying low. I do not want to die yet
because I am afraid I will meet her in the afterlife...
It is too soon. I have not grieved.

Maybe I should take up betting on horses
on Sunday afternoons. Or trap shooting, donating blood,
maybe golf or some other game they play at country clubs.

Something to take my mind off the emptiness
at the other end of the line.

Maybe I should have had a phone installed
in her shiny pecan casket.

When I was a child she baked my birthday cakes
and sewed my dresses like a grandmother in a fairy tale,
but she must have been in her own personal grief, one
husband lost in the war,
her son going mad, pickled in ideas of what it might mean to
be a Southern Gentleman,
her next husband having just succumbed young to cancer,
when he had promised her,
Promised her, she emphasized, he would not die first.

Later she told us how she would retreat to her closet to talk to
her late husband,
and it was hard to imagine what solace she found in that
small darkness.

After she was gone,
in that same closet I uncovered a luminous window
I vaguely remembered from childhood,
long buried behind generations of clothes,
suitcases of cards and letters of condolence,
the fur coats of the past blocking all the light,
a head with tiny mink teeth,
gripping its own tail.

October 16th, One Year Ago

One year ago to this day I arrived in Pennsylvania, a long
drive below a pink sky,
and suddenly we were in the East and there were tollbooths
not just any tollbooths
but a toll that cost seventeen dollars and I always wondered
what happens if you
just plain do not have the money?

So then we got to the house and we hugged the dog who was
as happy to see us as
we were to see him and now he is dead and gone.
Dear dog who carried my story,
my primary companion this past year, has gone on without
me. I know not where, and how he departed made no sense
either.
What path was that?
I whistle into the darkness.

But I remember then I took a long hot bath and washed off
the week of grime, soaked in the steam, and felt full of the
bison and the elk, the bubbling geysers, the red hills, the frost
dawn, the inland sea and the tall sand dunes, the antelope and
the purple sky with the moon like an old beach pebble in it,

And then I went to bed and began the year of not sleeping.

Reincarnation

The day after he died
I really thought it was your brother
turned up on the porch as a praying mantis
looming in the purple flowers.

You say this thought scares you,
this giant dinosaur insect scares you,
and I ask "Don't you have anything to say to your brother?"
and you say,
"Goodbye."

Eight Deaths, No Particular Order

You were the first to go, and I kissed you, your body smaller
than my face.
Nature was taking you back from me, and I felt the ancient
sorrow, a cave at the beginning of time.

You are not alive to see this yellow moon in all its fullness.
The first full one since you died in your sleep.
An autumn moon, a harvest moon,
it burns cold on this blue night.

Someone else is underground.
She sleeps and above her a lily bows its head with gravity.
A whippoorwill calls out; his kind is going extinct also.
Some day there will just be feathers, floating in museums.

Last night I was crying thinking about our last supper.
We ate in a western restaurant with a fireplace, giant salads
with blue cheese and onions,
you liked the dressing. I had forgotten this night. When we
had breakfast together I had felt your mortality, but that night
at dinner there was nothing mortal about us.
It was as if we washed down our meal with the wine of
eternity, the wine of denial.

Sometimes I find your fur beneath the piano, beneath the bed.
Now it mixes with the new puppy's fur and floats around on
little ghost feet.
I think of you holding up the earth, rolling in circles in the
green of day,
reveling in what was now, not thinking of what was to come.

Your death was sudden and as unexpected as all the others.
Hard to plan a funeral, whispers of foul play, black magic,

we found that more than one woman was claiming you as
hers.
Wife, sisters, then a girlfriend surfaced. You would be
divided in memory.
We would not quite know what to think.
There was nothing left to say.
And no opportunity left to say it.

Somehow I did not grieve you as hard as some.
I had been on vacation when gangrene followed your
dementia,
A freaky second act, but I was oblivious, not knowing you
were in hospital,
I actually thought you were inside our taxi driver, smiling at
me, your superb British accent, your happiness, as you told
me how long you had lived in Bermuda, "I take me tea at The
Parakeet, every afternoon. I love that and me cornmeal
porridge." I could not wait to get home and tell the family,
that I saw you,
you were off traveling in the theater of the world, and you
were free.

What is left of the other you?
Two gold eyes glowing in the dark of my memory.

Parts Unknown

The deaths were beginning to take something out of me
Each time someone was buried
I felt part of me was leaving too

Part of me was going underground
Part of me was in the coffin

Part of me was burned to ashes
Part of me was put in a box
Part of me was flung to the four winds

Part of me was lost

Finis

It was when we realized that our days were really numbered.

The same week I had read in the NY Times that there are
actually a limited number of stars that can be seen from earth
at any one time. Six thousand and something.
It didn't matter to me. I always get an eyeful.

When I was a child the stars used to lift me up out of myself.
The world was darker then.
We lived in the forests at the edge of fairytales.

I did not want us to leave each other.
It was getting harder every day to stay.
We took turns holding on.

When we looked at each other,
we were forced to look away.
We had seen each other too often in cemeteries.
We had viewed each other over too many caskets.

It even seemed like it was not *us* letting go
but like some force was prying our fingers apart
One by one

Until we were losing each other
and just gripping the air
where we had once been.

I found my own hands turned often to silent fists.

Ashes, ashes, we all fall down.

Master Cylinder

I did not know what it was
until it failed.

Like so many things
taken for granted

on a daily basis.

Worm

Sometimes you find a worm
writhing on the earth,
is it trying to get out?
Or get back under?
Some things are unclear.

Fly Away Home

Shiny rat-faced rage comes to visit
  runs over the wheel I am strapped to
        and gnaws out my eyeballs
like they were leftover Easter jellybeans.

  I had always thought
in the tall grass of summer
              I would find myself
        or be found.
That beneath my candy red carapace
      would unfold the wings of the ladybug
      "Ladybug ladybug, fly away home,
        your house is on fire, your children are burned,"
but instead I'm upside down,
kicking at death,
    perhaps Dying.

At The Sound of the Silence

I run screaming.

You should see what death has done to my hair.
You should see what it has done to my face,
I feel that a child with finger-paints
has gotten a hold of my soul.
Everything seems to be filled with rain.
The whole world a piñata full of pain.

"Don't swing your bat at me," I tell death.
Don't swing your bat at me.

I hear the music that gives one the dread,
the musical chairs music, the not so fun fun-house music.
Music that suggests we are all clowns, sad clowns.
The music that says
'This music will be interrupted by silence.
At the sound of the silence there will be one less chair.'

Push and shove, push and shove,
Even those you love.

No Chair Left for You

In my head Simon and Garfunkel are singing,
"I get all the news I need from the weather report,"
and what I have is even better than that.
I have the actual rain. It won't let up.
I walk outside barefoot and my feet get pricked by the holly
leaves.
Wake-up acupuncture in the dark.

Thunder and lightning, the world disappears and then
reappears,
hardly anything rearranged. But there is a little suspense.
Keep watching.
Next time maybe something will have been moved.
Maybe it will be musical chairs.
Maybe there will be no chair left for you.

Rant, Tarantula

I am so tired I want to eat my own face.
In the kitchen below I am baking
heart-shaped cookies
for dogs.

For a friend's dog who is sick with cancer,
who now gets chemo once a month,
a thing that seems it is made of spiders and their venom.

My own feelings arrive as if by train wreck.

I want to find that place where I belong
beside the pond, next to the nest of bees
whose thoughts all turn to honey.

Little bees who bury themselves in flowers, and as if
reincarnated they fly home, weighted down with gold.

When I am old,
which seems like a place I will reach soon,
I will pay attention to only these hidden hives,
the aquamarine aquariums of our minds.
Counting the fleeting sheep,
the dreaming bees.

Grief

Our grief tries
to make a pearl of us.

How we resist.

Coffin, Hatchet

Who doesn't eat death for breakfast?

Even my kind vegan brother beheads
the oats of morning.

Rage comes, and later it breaks your arm.
Death always wins with its sneaky arm-wrestling moves

Death, the undefeated champ
My old friend

You say denial
I say "tomahto"

Not just Uncharted territory
But unchartable territory

If the past was a coffin,
The future was a hatchet.

We had lost even our tongues

I have been to the ocean and back,
losing my feet when the waves came in.
Returning home, I found my pillow turned to
ashes. We no longer hungered for bread.
The dog would lie at the feet we no longer had
and not only had the coals in the fireplace grown cold
but there was no longer a fireplace at all.

It was a modern scene.
It was as if someone was doing a painting in reverse.

Soon there would be a blank canvas.
Mysteriously the next person who would come along,
would choose oils, would paint a scene
of a man and a woman and a
yellow dog walking along a beach.

When we lay down, we did not get up again.
We had lost even our tongues.

Postcard

I write to you from my own personal Pompeii.
Things are made of ashes. People are frozen in the position
they had their last happy thought. Their last taste of dinner.
Their last kiss.
Surely some were reduced to ash while smoking.
Some were expecting other things to happen.

Mother the Earth

When we bury the mother,
we bury the earth in the earth.

The one we came here through.
Tunnel and womb, in whom,
we made our bones, our hands,
our feet, our eyes.
Perhaps our first ideas.

The one whose blood and milk
gave us life.

We spent her
as we spent our lives.

She grew light.

We set her down upon the earth,
the best we knew how.

For Grandma Nancy 1927-2008

Solar Power

It is hot, one feels like the inside of the body
might just ooze out to the outside,
like one might fall down inside oneself,
like one might finally dissolve and become
one with the world.

The world is like being inside a hot mitten.
It's jungle tropical hot and we turn extraordinary shades of
red,
not from sunburn just from the rosy plumping of our
capillaries
and every pore opened like little windows.

The playground is empty.
The bbq sits abandoned.
I have never seen the neighborhood so still.

A tiny breeze comes like a coke-cola,
the pause that refreshes,
 as I watch turtles bake their old bones.
We reflect, as we are reflected upon.

Death is the ultimate back stage

Sometimes I am so weirded out by a certain emptiness in the air. I cannot call my grandmother now and thank her for the world book encyclopedias which she bought for me in 1974 and which I inherited when she died last year in 2006. There is a smiling dog I loved who died this year and his tail wags in my brain. There was another dog and now we have his golden retriever cousin and the dogs have started to overlap in my mind. There is a friend whose hand I sometimes feel on my shoulder. A friend I still tried to email a month after he was gone. A woman I still want to write letters to, to confide in. I can hear her laugh and sweet voice. All these people who have faded into some place, I wish I could hit the back key, flip the calendar back and visit them, on those pages they still live on, the pages of the past.

We ache.

I pay more attention to the rain than I used to.
The sound of the cicada disappears and reappears,
partly a cello in the night, partly a violin.
The fireflies reflect the luminous moon.
There are frogs calling out for each other
from the far ends of the vast wet universe.

I miss laughter more and when I hear it I am delighted.
It has more value than gold.
It is the pearl made in the human heart
from the times when we ache
and are all the same.

No One Ever Really Dies

The light breaks off in different ways down here,
colors I have never seen,
like the air is made of tinted glass,
rainbows, refractions, falling light.

The eye is a kaleidoscope.

What do you think, I am lying dead?
That in decomposition these are the spectral hallucinations
I have as moles eat my eyes. They feast; I am still and calm
dreaming between the dirt sheets?

You may be right.

The old me,
renews the new me.

She will come up flowers.

I saw Heath Ledger standing with his back to me.
He looked groggy and was knocking at a door
to get let back in, like a sleepwalking man
who locks himself out of the house.

Up above Britney Spears is expressing
a kind of condolence,
in her British accent what she says is,

"He's still here. Oh, yes.
No one ever really dies. No one."

Trying to write about it

It happens in darkness, a warm sweet darkness,
in soft blankets
when we find each others bodies with our hands and not our
eyes,

An ancient reaching made new again.
We are sleep-deprived like new parents,
only there are no children.

We have been the midwives of death.
My pet, my friend, my grandmother, our dog, your brother,
like a line of dominos,

and suddenly we lived in a house of cards.
So the bed is like the raft we reach each night,
it is the little bit of land where we find comfort

and reaching into each other, it is hard to say what happens
but reassuring to know it can happen without effort.
Your head on my chest, our legs pressed close,
openings and closings,
something rhythmic and old breathes life into us.

Orbiting the earth from my room upstairs

Winter and
the world is a rock hard diamond
a chunk of ice who wears us on its finger
but not on its ring finger.

Today when the sun came out the world began turning to
mud.
We wore it on the bottoms of our shoes,
we tracked the outdoors indoors,
the dog brought it in.

Downstairs my mate pulled the ghost of Beethoven out of the
piano,
that old piano who was once a tree in a forest of others,
once just standing around.

And I sit up in my nest.
If the house vanished from beneath me,
it would appear that I was floating in the air
just orbiting the earth,

Here next to this oak tree
next to these birds,

looking down on the earth
looking down.

The Jail of the Ordinary

Slept through the deep rumbling
of the thunder
as if I were buried deep in a bear's belly

but rose to curtains of rain falling.
Couldn't see past the windows
and the world became blessedly small
and simple.

Tea, poems.
The dog slept through the
high whistling of the kettle.

When the storm stopped,
it was as if a rain bomb had gone off.

But the birds began to chatter
fluffing up their feathers

And I knew soaked seeds would soon
be sprouting and reaching cloudward

After our nap,
all of us trying to break back into
the jail of the ordinary.

Crumbs of Hope

Some people have a cross
or meditation beads or a smooth stone,

Some people jangle their coins ceaselessly.

In my pocket
I have a dog biscuit
and I touch it silently
to see that it is still there.

Object of hope that there might be a chance encounter at the
beach
someone might show up at the edge of the woods

Or in the heart of the yard in the late moonlight
and I will be prepared.

Eulogy/Sorrow and Thanksgiving

We let you go
With sorrow and thanksgiving

This is the job of the living.

Let there be no fear
In your death
With your death

May you go gently
With singing

With someone's gentle hands
On your bones

With the quiet passing of the
Winds over the fields
Of grasses
Humming a little

Letting you go
A little

We let you go
with sorrow and thanksgiving.

This is the job of the living.

Fish cannot leave deep waters,

And a country's weapons should not be displayed.

Lao Tsu

Thirty-Six
Tao Te Ching

Letters from Underground

I.

I worry that there is no place for me above ground,
having nearly died so many times
one loses interest in the world of men.

One finds that the pomegranates are sweet
that garnets sparkle like sunlight.
There is an inner sunlight to be found down here,

If one looks,
and keeps looking.

II.

I surface occasionally in moonlight.
Sometimes dogs come out of the shadows and follow me,

Cats too,
as if our journey smells of fishes,
of green grass, and promises.

When we part company
we have each marked our corners
in our own ways,
and may find our way back
when time stands still.

We mark this life, for the afterlife.

III.

Death is the place where time stands still.

They say death stops for no man
but they are wrong

Death stops instead
for every man,

Even the child knows this.

This is even what the dog says
when it runs in speedy circles on the lawn
stirring up all the molecular joy that can be had on this earth,

the only earth there is.

The Pear Tree

Our ritual is this~
We run through the autumn rain
to the pear tree
which is so laden with fruit
we think of ourselves as almost charitable
relieving its boughs of the weight
which is threatening to crack it in two,
split its limbs from its body.

The rain is thick and chilly.
The dog's body so golden running over lush neglected grass,
like a river of gold,
 rushing over a river of green.

We each grab a pear
and then turn and run,
fast as we can,
back to the house.
I am a child again.

Once inside the door,
the dog cheerfully greedily grabs at both pieces of fruit.
His smiling jaws leaving tooth marks in our quarry, he
steals mine while I am drying his paws with a towel.

What can I say that he will understand?
I say nothing and wait for tomorrow
when I will be quicker, when I will be smarter.

September 8th

The puppy runs beneath the full moon, jauntily he carries a stick from the sycamore tree, he struts in the moonlight like he has won first prize. What does he care? His is a world of naps and chew toys and strange new treats. He does not know that he will be neutered in a few months. That he will not be a show dog for anything but freedom and joy. At the park with the Alice in Wonderland benches he digs down to the roots of the grass like he has found dog watercress, or truffles.

Sometimes this makes him so delirious with joy he tucks his tail between his legs and runs so fast in circles that he appears to be a molecule of water about to boil, or an ad for nuclear energy. His lips blow back from the wind his running creates. His whole body is all smiles.

And those watching are all smiles too, we duck and dash out of the way as his steering mechanism does not work at high speed.

My love and I hold hands, actually we do not, but we are so equally tired that we are at peace with this, and it gives one the sense that one is holding hands.

Nearby the ducks sleep on the water, silently floating tufts of feathers.

Puppy in the Rain

We are in my childhood again.
The world is simple as the label of a Morton salt shaker.
We have no umbrella,
and we splash in the puddles,
see ourselves upside down
until we are washed away by the mud.

And here he is, puppy new to this earth,
just 14 weeks of living
while I have 37 years of memories
and stood bedside while the last dog died, quickly,
prematurely
and where the ashes sit on the shelf~
the new puppy sniffs at the pinecones
and shells from the last walk taken with other dog.

They never knew each other.
Like blades of grass,
these little puppies sprout up.
They don't know each other, their lives are so short
but they manufacture joy like the fur they shed all over the
house.

My grandmother just died.
The house contains a trunk that belonged to my great Aunt.
In it is her college diploma from 1909, (no small feat)
and her bloomers, and her hair.
Right now, we are afraid to look any further.

Safe

The small clocks still tick.
Your watch is running on my dresser,
a year after your death
though it's not going anywhere.
It measures I know not what.

You have been safely deposited in your pecan coffin.
An embalmed figure who was last seen
wearing a yellow pantsuit
and holding a winning hand of cards.

And your diamond ring,
the one we removed after you turned blue
and left behind your hands, your wrists,
if you are ever looking for it,
it is in the safe deposit box at the bank.

The key is in the desk upstairs,
top drawer on the right,
safe like you would like it.

Conundrum

Walking the beach again I am reminded
that I do believe in something
bigger, older than us,

Something not manmade.
Perhaps we did make ourselves, and that is why god is in our image
but we did not make everything else.

Perhaps each species simply has its own god
like an elected official.

I just care for the god of stones and circuses.

The ocean, the puppy,
Lions, monkeys, elephants
Flowers, clouds, trees, stones, moss, water, light…

My favorite things are not manmade,
why would my god be?

Next Generation

I wonder if the girls across the street are getting pregnant.
The way the boys flock in, I can smell them, I am not too old
yet to still smell them.
But I see that the parents are sweet and would have a
disbelief, that their girls could be
doing anything like that, that they console themselves saying
they let the kids all hang out there so they don't feel they
have to sneak around.

At night there are boys in the trees, silent simian shadows,
and there are the firefly-like flashes of cellphones,
things illuminated and sending each other signals.

I remember what that was like
to be all heat and light.

Hawaii Earthquake 6.5 October 2006

I call a friend day later to be certain he is fine and to see if he
 had a nice earthquake experience like that time I had in
Seattle when the earth rolled
like a giant cat standing up to stretch and the dog and I went
into the street and
could see the dirt turned to waves.
We were so happy the earth was alive and our legs simply
rode the land the way one walks on a boat in deep seas.

He calls back to tell me that when it struck he was outside
looking for a cat
who had run off having sensed the approaching quake.
He stood under swaying trees and could see the house as it
shook like a rug.
"More tremors today," he said, "everyone was ok.
Mainly there was just broken glass,
broken statues of Buddha and Krishna,
and then a lightning storm."

The poem may be full of clichés
but the earth is not.

The Dog Tooth-Fairy

Tonight baby dog lost his first tooth
and I wonder if the dog tooth-fairy will come?

He is so soft I feel like I am petting sand or butter or velvet.
His ears are like rabbit fur.

He was chewing his whelping toy when I glanced down
and saw blood on the sheepskin and then heard
something clatter on the floor.

It was a tiny bloody tooth, a white shark tooth.

I kissed his head and stroked his fur,
and felt like crying, little fellow and his milestones.
For a moment it was like having a baby
and I talked to him in English
because we are all turning into crazy people,
aren't we?

I even wondered if the tooth-fairy would come.

I had been watching his teeth since the night before.
The old teeth were being pushed out by the new tooth so
aggressively
you could almost see it happening before your eyes.
It looked painful,
but he seemed to go along with it uncomplainingly,
like he believed in god better than I did.
That there was a plan
and he would just chew sticks
until the time was past.

I stroked his ears
and wanted to get him a present for what he had lost.

Two Dogs

No day could have been more beautiful,
the first day of Fall and the air warm and the sky gold and
blue.

You were both dead
so I took your ashes to the beach
and scattered them like stardust at the edge of the sea,
between the moon and sun which were both shining like
happy baldheaded twins
on opposite ends of a seesaw.

I scattered shells and stones we had picked up on walks.
Losing you was bitter and made life an impenetrable unripe
fruit,
not once, but twice.

But I did not stay long for we have a new puppy now
and he was waiting in the car. Our pockets were full of tiny
bones,
training treats, and we would run him further up the coast,
where he could go off-leash.

Death you kept catching up to me,
like a rogue wave that grabs your legs when your back is to
the sea,
but we were determined to keep leaving footprints, run
splashing into you,
even as you erased us, bit at our bare heels.

As I drove to the beach I listened to Buena Vista Social Club,
because it is the most beautiful Sad music, because I do think
sad music is its own genre,
and it was played by men who were quite old
and now have joined you at the edges of time.

My mind was filling up with sunset and the smell of autumn
and the sound of crickets
but one part was chastising me a little, saying
Wait, we are in modern times, to be a success is being
something like a CEO,
practice managing time like it is a clock, make mountains of
money,
organize people like they have moveable parts and snap-off
replaceable heads,

When instead I am someone who has a long list today which
read:
Plant the allium and the grape hyacinth and daffodil bulbs so
Spring will bring color, sprinkle the dog's ashes, write a
poem, dust the corners, eat the mints left from the funeral
home, make sure there are seeds for the birds, transcribe the
old family letters, think about how the dogs ran in happy
circles and spilled over with joy,
Such that the world still has puddles of joy one can fall into.

The dogs and I are kindred.

The waves roll in and out,
even while we are sleeping.

(Fall Equinox September 2007, Sea Bright NJ, for Gabe and Max)

Third Anniversary

Full moon and a bouquet of
magnolia blooms

harvested from a tree cut down
lying in the ditch
tossed out.

Our hands meet.
Our lips meet.
The house is heavy with perfumes.

The floor littered with petals.

Harvesting the Day

There is something in each day that matters, and I want to
capture it, to gather it, to harvest the days, panning for the
gold of certain moments, the thing that reflects sunlight, the
amber that hardens and holds the fossil record of the day.

We must become the most interesting people we can.

I find the flower, the little white trumpet that emits such
sweetness.
It is an old fairytale fragrance,
ah that is what woods smell like,
fairy perfume, a mythological ambrosia that makes you
forget we are at war,
that there is the stench of bodies decaying not that far away.
A five year old Iraqi boy was burned into a mass of scar
tissue by two strangers who doused him with gasoline and
fled.
His mother fainted when she saw him, and now she wonders
why he is so bitter,
though she knows, and says death would be better than the
life they all have now.

I walk the path beneath the buttonwoods and must admit, I
try to let the story slip from my mind, a tear of salt, an ocean
of news.

The dog calls us out of ourselves.

The dog found its kinship with the carnivore.

What is innocence?

Who sharpened the bee's stinger?

Next to me the grass is lush and soggy, mist coats my skin,
my thoughts.
My own path today is one of serenity, a gold dog on a red
leash, rain, and nowhere I have to be. Or go.

How white the osprey and how green his prey.

How slippery the fish and how smooth the water.

How the pond without ripples barely reflects a sky without
clouds.

As I walk the path home,
I was so glad to be born into the time of the sycamores.
Now if only there were a way to make something,
to be as industrious as bees,
as trees, as leaves.

Home Medicine

Because I was slightly afraid that he might die, I made him a couple of peanut butter and honey sandwiches and fed them to him. Then I let him eat the bookmark he found on the table, and a clean white Kleenex that fell from the empty box like a ghost. If he had found a hundred dollar bill I might have let him eat it. I watched him closely. It was a rainy day and I had opened the back door so he could go outside and pee. I turned my back and steeped a cup of tea and when I turned around again he was lying happily in the wet grass eating a piece of metal drain pipe. 'He cannot be eating that,' I thought as I went outside, 'it is made of metal,' flooded with that mother's worst fear that it was not just metal but covered in lead paint. When I approached him and traded for a cookie indeed he seemed to have chewed off the edges like it was gum. How much had he swallowed? Had he swallowed? It was hard to see what he had spit out in the wet thick grass. I brought him inside and tried to measure the missing edge against my finger, making a straight line to see what was missing. It was hard to say. The puppy just smiled. It was a hundred dollars just to show up at the vet hospital. I went to make him another sandwich. He seemed to especially like the organic blueberry jam.

Lunch Break at the Pond

When we approached the pond we saw that the great blue
heron was standing taller than usual,
stretching its sharp head skyward,
and then we saw that its neck was also distended,
in an odd stiff way
and it sort of silently half coughed and we saw the flash of a
tail or a fin in its mouth.

And the heron seemed to want to fly away
but too much was going on.
What does that feel like to have lunch flipping around in your
throat,
fighting you so hard
as it resists sliding into your belly?

And it became clear that the great blue heron had flown over
here to the pond,
just the way one swings by a favorite café for a sandwich at
lunchtime.

Only lunch for the heron was obviously a dangerous time, for
you could be attacked
by a girl and a dog while you were busy grappling
with a large fish who was stuck in your throat
and preventing you from flying off.

And as it wrestled with its meal
the bird did what any sensible being would do.
We watched as it drank some water,
and then it drank some more.

Cicada Song

What are the cicadas saying?
Do they even know? I wonder if like our own species they
are just half drunk
on the sound of themselves, just repeating old stories they
once heard,
something they picked up underground.

Around the world there are over two thousand species of
cicadas,
do they know this about themselves?
Do they know that humans call them "Black Prince" and
"Cherrynose."
"Green Grocer," "Yellow Monday," and "Red Eye"?

That the world is so colorful.

That in human history, the cicada was sacred to Apollo,
a Greek symbol of resurrection and mortality?

What do they know that we don't?

And how long will their species go on singing
and how long will my species go on listening,
or noticing at all?

Utah Mine Collapse August 2007

Above ground someone is practicing Chopin on a piano
and a girl is making a caramel cake.
There are cicadas screeching in the night,
in the branches of the tallest oak trees.

We are underground where it is silent,
the cave collapsed above us and the darkness
filled our very pores.
It is dark in our eyes, dark deep down into our lungs,
our thoughts too are growing dark.

People thought it was an earthquake but it was us,
this practice of retreat mining
of blowing up the ceiling behind us as we go.
A way to extract the very last bit of what we came here for.

Up above a child is laughing, another one taking a nap,
I dare not think about our own children, my own child.

Six of us down here where there is no sound,
so dark we could be upside down,
and what is left of the oxygen
can only be divided so far.
One slice of apple pie
amongst a nation starving for hope.

Toeprint

I want to hear that they have found the miners
so I keep turning on the tv.

I know it is impossible that they are still alive,
the earth kept shifting.
The mine owner said the cave-in was from an earthquake
but the seismologists said what registered as an earthquake
was the collapse of the mine as it fell.

The economics of the mine operator, I am sure he feels that
rumbling.
Last year they were cited for thirty violations.

If the six men did survive, it would have been a dark
miserable hell
with minimal oxygen.

People lit candles up on the surface
and they burned deep into the night.

I turn on the news to find a man in Sierra Leone whose arms
were chopped off
by a rebel fighter less than ten years ago.
This man did not give up, and when it came time to vote,
he voted with a toeprint.

The Hague is now trying people like Charles Taylor
and hoping to establish a rule of law.

Cantaloupe

It's morning underground and I am cutting the cantaloupe
while I am listening to the sad bitter rhyming words of
Eminem
and what music of the spheres did the cantaloupe hear
as it grew in the field and was plucked there in Virginia
and I drove by and paid a few bucks for it, using
the bills with the pictures of my ancestor George on them,
and now here on my sacrificial altar in the kitchen in New
Jersey, the fruit
begins its reincarnation to these lyrics from "When I'm
Gone"

"and when I'm gone, just carry on, don't mourn
rejoice every time you hear the sound of my voice…"

and I remember how I loved the wordplay of childhood,
how cantaloupe could be broken into the words
'Can't elope'
whatever that meant.

One grows up and learns that the language of adults
is the language of the military.
One hears that 'clear to engage' means free to fight and kill.
I get so confused by who is the enemy.

But I loved the way words were sweet and meaty with sound
and meaning
like ripe fruit in season in the South.

Tomatoes and figs, strawberries and wild cherries,
tomorrow always bursting forth.
The land was our grocery store.
It seemed the earth produced just for us.

Melons are sometimes compared to human body parts,
breasts and heads,
but the body is tougher and bounces back, again and again.
The melon grew in wind and rain and it died by gleaming
knife and rap music
though some would say it is already inert, disconnected from
its vine and roots,
its earth.

But the journey continues on,
The teeth, the tongue.

Face Down with My Fate

I.

How did I become this person
who lies naked face down on a table
while another person rubs hot stones
over my back, healing my broken shoulder blades.

It works and it seems to have existed as medicine
long before doctors, long before insurance companies,
and the crisis in health care.

We went to the woman who lived in the mists
near the geysers and volcanoes where she
ironed us out and then gave our bodies back to us
after we had been badly broken by an animal
we were hunting. Our dinner.

The practitioner is half Oneida, an enrolled tribal member,
"Though," she says, "the Oneida are a dying breed."

II.

I was so strong, how did I become the injured?
It did not happen with one tremendous tear.
Just the cumulative burden-the overstretched reach—
And I could no longer take to air.

III.

I broke my back on the world.

IV.

Who will eat me while I am down here on the ground?

V.

I find my hands at the bottoms of my arms
in tight balls, twisting my shoulders inward.
Soon I may no longer walk upright.

I always did have such long arms.
It encouraged me to pluck the furthest fruits.

Who grew me?

Who goes there?

The Chiropractor

I don't like him or the way he looks at me or the way he talks to me, I have more rapport with the life-sized skeleton hanging there in the corner. But after he applies the heat and the electricity to my broken wing, after he holds my neck and cracks it, saying 'this will be loud because it is close to your eardrums,' saying 'I have you,' and twisting my neck so it sounds like a string of firecrackers set off by small boys long after Independence Day, after

I come away smelling like weird liniment, like I have been bathed in blue chalky menthol, I can see more clearly, can think better, can move more of my body, turn my neck to look at the sunflowers, some of whose heads have broken their own stalks with the weight of their seeds, and hang down as if they are grieving.

I still don't like him but I am grateful. Apparently this was what I needed, for someone I do not even like to take my neck between their hands and crack it. Hard.

Chiro II.

"I have you," he says again, as he twists my neck and my spine and my bones crackle like poprocks in the salivating mouth of my fate. Pain brought me here, and hope keeps me here. The treatment gets more complex, at one moment he has a hold of my arms, and one leg, and in other rooms this could almost be kama sutra like, but here we are all business and he rearranges me with a quick tug and then helps me up by cradling my neck and telling me to get up and walk around.
When the vibrating machine is applied to me I feel first like a wooden floor being polished for a masked ball, sunk happily and sleepily below the floorboards. The next machine makes me a pond of water at an old mill where a helicopter is just about to land.

There are moment when I am not sure he is not injecting something into my shoulder, my neck, is that searing heat and release really just the Novocain of well applied pressure and not some old quack medicine a man sold out of wagons? But I decide I will not stop him, part of the treatment is trust, and when I found my way to this office, I was like a wounded bear coming upon a cottage of humans in the woods, and falling on their doorstep with an arrow in my back.
In my time of need they saved me, and so my ferocious wild skeptical control freak side calms down and something in me begins to become the pet. I domesticate. I have no choice.

When I leave the office and catch my own eyes in the rear view car mirror, I feel
I can see straight into myself, that my bones and flesh are getting along better, that the wild animal who is me has been satisfied, and is resting, has found its stillness.

Eating The Animal

Now when I taste meat, I taste the animal.
This is my intention.

We will all someday be eaten by death, eaten by time,
we will be its delicious drive-thru cheeseburger.
We will drip with salt and juice.
We will be a thing death licks off its fingers.

We will fill the things belly.

Time too will erase us,
a chalkboard in one of the classrooms
of your childhood.
Maybe your fifth grade chalkboard,
maybe your first.

Were you ever called upon to beat the erasers?
How they formed a choking chalk dust cloud
everything stirred up together,
all the lessons and all the answers swirling in the air.

The time was coming,
I would lie down again with lions, the rough tongue of my
fate.
Dragged there by my neck, I would not be breathless, failing
to have run.
There would be that deafening purring, that pre death
massage by a carnivore's tongue.
My blood the lion's little glass of port after a nice wildebeest
roast and maybe just a few delicate blades of grass from the
hooves, the pursuit.

It was my life, I would have cherished every moment of it.

The Mulberry Tree

I go there because it is there,
because it is the best thing that New Jersey has to offer,
it is what is left of the original earth.

We walk down the sidewalk and meet a mom whose belly is
swollen like a small round melon is growing in her. Or has a
beach ball washed up inside her?
She declares that my puppy is as cute as the dickens
while her blonde toddler pretends to mow the lawn with a
plastic toy mower.

I have been driven to the woods by the sound of real mowers.

We pass two dogs who remind me that I meant to buy a gun
when I was in Virginia.
For as they leap and snarl at us through the fence that is too
low, I look to see what house I will run to for help.
I know no one. Who will answer and will they save us?

I tell the puppy, "stay with me," and we walk as briskly and
far away as possible.
The white dog nearly makes it over but I am not afraid of the
white one.
He sometimes half wags his tail as he lunges. But now that
he is almost over just as gravity's joke on him,
I do worry that he will be so shocked to have escaped that he
will bite us, just trying to figure out who he is.

No, it is the Rottweiler I am afraid of. Aren't they beautiful?
Don't they look like they were made to kill and eat grizzly
bears? The way this one leaps and lunges, I know if the white
one gets over, this one will follow, and I feel the adrenaline
surge into my legs and then subside, leaving me shaky.

We get by but I vow to not return this way.

At the park, there too a man on a riding mower is mowing the grass.

We eat honeysuckle in the shade and then interrupt the mower's pattern to stand in the center of the field and pluck firm berries from the branches where high above birds are singing and feasting also.

We don't have our fill but we have enough.

We head home through a thick forest full of vining things, honeysuckle, grapes, and poison ivy.

We are struck by the seriousness in which a family is looking at the sides of their house. It is hard for me to tell if they are now comparing two shades of gray or two shades of tan and I am not sure either color can really stand so much scrutiny.

Oh I see, they are switching to tan. And which shade of tan is better? The man says with authority, "Now remember it may lighten up."

This is the year that half the neighborhood has gone tan. With black shutters and trim.
It is a smart look, when one or two houses do this.

It is not nearly so nice when everyone does. And I have to wonder, does every family stand outside alone, studying two shades of tan like life depended upon it?

Didn't anyone just say, "I'll have what they have?" pointing to every other house in the neighborhood.

At the pond we see the hawk again and a red-winged
blackbird.
Last week we were amazed to see the blackbird drive away
the hawk by pecking at its head.

Today, there is the hawk again and the blackbird is flying
along below it and I think wow, it is driving it off again,
when I have one of those "expectation violations"
as the hawk barely moves but reaches and grasps the song
bird in its clutches. The hawk flies off like it is carefully
carrying a small fish.

And with that, the red-winged blackbird sings no more.

It must all depend on who is on top.

Yesterday I was startled to see, on Sycamore Avenue at the
Trinity Episcopal Church in Little Silver, right next to a busy
intersection,
a hawk sitting on a gravestone.

Perched there on the top of a curved stone like a raven in a
Poe poem. The bird was so silvery and still I thought for a
moment I was hallucinating, that it was stone come to life,
but the light was red so I got to sit and watch.
And there it sat. And I wondered whose grave that was.

This week when I walked I met a very obedient dog and I
commented on what a well-behaved dog the woman had and
she nicely replied, "Well he had better be good,
I am his trainer."

And so the world goes on.

Hive

Yesterday on our walk we found a beehive
a great humming nest of bees in the hollow of the sycamore
tree.
Does this happen anymore?
It seems so old fashioned, bees in a tree,
like we had stumbled into Christopher Robin's Hundred-
Acre Wood,
walked back into childhood, that the beast on the other end of
the leash was really Winnie-The-Pooh.

But here we are in urban New Jersey,
and the bees took over a hollow
and built their empire facing the pond, their backs to the
road, suburban busybodies,
just like everyone else.

***

Twice this week the bees have invaded my dreams,
Both times stinging me, bashing into my subconscious and
repeating the lessons they undoubtedly told my cave dwelling
ancestors:
Give us some space, find your own hollow tree,
Find your own flowers, make your own honey.

The Fish Hawk

We walk in the rain and the world is all ours.
As the pond rises, so do the ducks,
so does our happiness.

We are in time to catch yet one more miraculous act in the
food chain theater
a white hawk, whom I had thought was a red tail,
circles the pond three times and for a moment I am not sure if
it is after the ducks, or after us, and again I am glad that I am
not any smaller,
that my dog is not any smaller, or else we would take cover
when it swoops so low and slow that we can see the
sharpness of its feathers,
the pool of its eye.

When it plunges, it stuns us, how it dives into the water
until entirely submerged, we dare not blink
and then with raptor speed it flies back toward the sky
a green fish in its talons,
and I can't help but think what the view is like to this fish
as the hawk which I now suspect is a sea hawk, a fish hawk,
an osprey,
circles up to the tops of the trees,
it doesn't even land for a bit,
but spirals upward in the rain
as if showing this fish the one glimpse of the whole world
that it will ever get.

(for Rilke)

I Spy

I spy on the old man
because I am intrigued by his bookshelves.
On the way to the beehive I pass the old man's house.

Tonight in the rain the bees are sleeping
but the old man is watching Seinfeld reruns
including the commercials.

He sits on his sofa in front of the bookshelves,
the background I am so transfixed by
and he watches TV alone.

I might have once upon felt sorry for him,
worried or lonely for him, but now I believe
that being alone and getting to organize one's own time
can be the greatest adventure, a solid joy.

Whenever he is outside, I say hello to him
and try to not interrupt his reverie as he rakes leaves,
do not want to startle him out of his aloneness.

Just want to let him know I am here,
If he ever wants to talk or
loan somebody his favorite book.

Surrounded by Distance

I carried no currency in this world.

In my pockets, room only for my hands.

It was my thoughts that jingled.
The world, and the walk we took,
was a little song.

"Near me nothing but distances."   Antonio Porchia

The houses were so close
as to be impossibly far apart.
Everyone averted their eyes at once.
It was as if the yards were infinite kingdoms.
Everyone lives inside invisible fences.

No neighbors from which to borrow
an egg or cup of sugar.

Two years later I would still not know their faces,
if I saw them in the store.

There are Latinos again, doing the lawns,
but they are not the same ones.
No, they don't all look alike.
So many people forced underground,
floating like ghosts, sweating like animals.

So many people and histories go into making us.

Finally the puppy is growing up.

He stops trying to eat my pen,
as I write to you.

Natural History

An oak leaf
falling onto a pine branch

Nature touches itself.
Is it all the same thing?

At the feeder
the red finches line up after the mourning doves.

Cardinals follow and
it's like someone touched them up with the same red
paintbrush.

A flicker on the tree in the backyard makes a noise
I heard when the red-headed woodpecker last visited.

The crow seems to have borrowed a line from the bullfrog.

The great egret is the full moon twin
of the blue heron who wades in and clutches a catfish,

whose whiskers I have seen on old men in the history of the
South.

My Mountain

From the cliffs where I stood in animal paths
waist high in the thorns, I saw Mount Baker today.
I do recall the years when I was so defeated that there was
nothing inside me that was still standing.

There are things smaller than us
that can destroy us.

I was a flat field of scorched nothingness.
Back then, I turned myself that direction
toward the mountain
My northstar, my polaris,
a bright spot that holds up the fixed sky
while all the stars and people spin around.
Morning comes, and comes again.

I was looking for nouns.
I found a mountain.
in fact, a volcano.

Koma Kulshan

There are things larger than us
that can restore us.

Lighthouse

Walking on the beach, today I made it around a peninsula.
I have not been able to navigate this tip in two years,
out of synch with the tides or something,
or the currents too powerful.

Just where I expected to turn around as usual, two elders
were coming toward me. I was thinking how I hoped I get to
grow old and be like them, all faded tennis shoes, beach hats,
wrinkles and smiles,
when they offered up this unsolicited encouragement,
The man said "You can do it," and the woman said.
"You just have to use the right timing."

And walking forward I rounded the fingertip of the land
without changing my pace or rhythm even a bit,
and Mount Baker was still there glowing, not distant at all.

Fort Worden State Park
Port Townsend, WA

More So

The earth is beautiful everywhere.
This time, dog-tooth violets, trout lilies, the tawny
woodpeckers.

This journey is sometimes one path and not the other.
Near the end we might find nothing was so dire,
Look, there is the mother, there is the lover. They are alive.
Nature asserts itself, drops the mirror that was just a
series of ripples at the watering hole
before the sun drank it all up.

All the possible paths in the world
cross themselves
once or twice

Not either or
But either *and*

Open your eyes wide enough.

The rapt woodpecker in the tree
oblivious to us standing below,
the dappled leaves rising out of the dirt.

Poem for the New Year (January 2015)

I became a tree, and my hands were birds.
It worked perfectly well.
And I had not even planned it,
or planned for it.

You never know what part of the road
will be filled with potholes,
and what part will be ribbon candy.

The owl is a thought the tree has.

Last night I smelled the North Pole coming all the way down
here to the Gulf Coast.
Everyone else was asleep.
It had a fragrance of cold stars and white bears,
rode the thermals like a flock of glittering swans, and flew
around the papaya tree,
and the palms.

In the dream, someone mentioned something
about their aorta.
I am not ready to think about that.
It seemed wise to read Raymond Carver stories, and prepare
to start again.

Maybe this will be the year you teach me how to play your
favorite song on the piano, and then I can play it for you,
the way you play Beethoven's Sonata Pathetique for me, the
music brought to life, before us, beyond us, and here we are,
beneath the sun and the moon. Spinning still.

Slowly. Slowly.

www.ingramcontent.com/pod-product-compliance
Lightning Source LLC
Chambersburg PA
CBHW032148020726
47496CB00003B/771